JAMAICA BAY PAMPHLET LIBRARY 04

JAMAICA BAY   FINDING ZERO

STRUCTURES OF COASTAL RESILIENCE

Jamaica Bay Team
Spitzer School of Architecture
The City College of New York

Catherine Seavitt Nordenson, editor
Associate Professor of Landscape Architecture

Kjirsten Alexander
Research Associate

Danae Alessi
Research Associate

Eli Sands
Research Assistant

JAMAICA BAY PAMPHLET LIBRARY
04 Jamaica Bay   Finding Zero

ISBN 978-1-942900-04-7

COPYRIGHT

CONTACT
Catherine Seavitt Nordenson
cseavittnordenson@ccny.cuny.edu
www.structuresofcoastalresilience.org

SCR Jamaica Bay Team
The City College of New York
Spitzer School of Architecture
Program in Landscape Architecture, Room 2M24A
141 Convent Avenue New York, New York 10031

COVER
Intertidal zone: contours -3 to +3 NAVD 88.

supported by

THE ROCKEFELLER FOUNDATION   SCR Structures of Coastal Resilience   CUNY The City University of New York   The City College of New York

THE IMPORTANT OF FINDING ZERO: DESIGN AND VERIFICATION

CREATING A MERGED DIGITAL ELEVATION MODEL

Land is continually shaped by water, particularly in the Jamaica Bay region where the sandy substrate erodes and accretes rapidly with both the dynamic flow of water and human activity.

Understanding the morphology of Jamaica Bay and its surroundings as a continuous surface is essential. Land can be visualized as a maleable vessel that holds constantly fluctuating amoungs of moving water—levels and current directions change daily with tides, periodically with storms, and steadily over the long term with sea level rise. This vision of the land and water allows for a design strategy that reflects these dynamic conditions and permits variable outcomes.

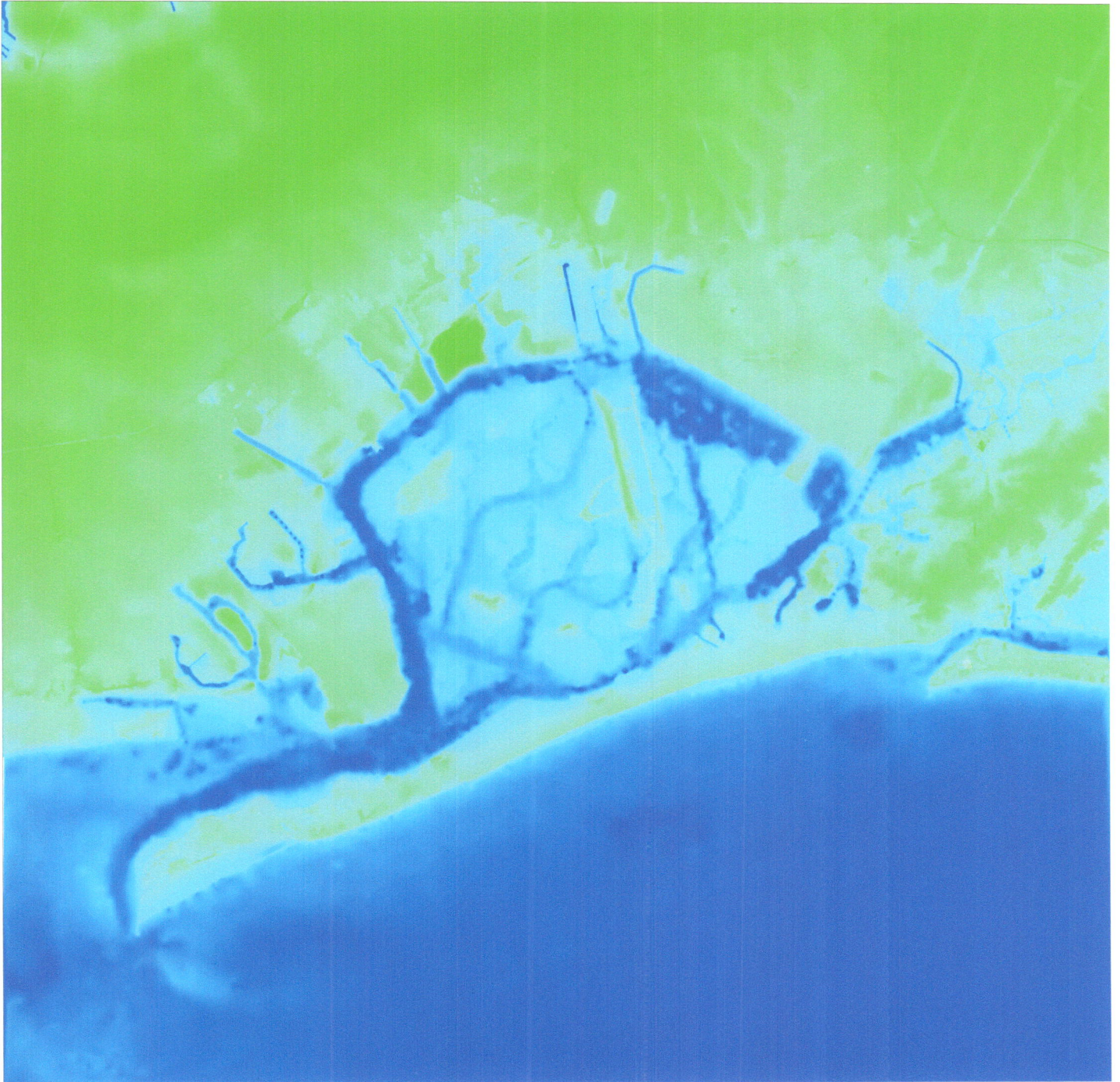

The Jamaica Bay topobathy is a Digital Elevation Model (DEM) merging topographic and bathymetric data.

THE IMPORTANT OF FINDING ZERO: DESIGN AND VERIFICATION

DESIGNING WITH TOPOGRAPHIC CONTOURS

The design interventions in this project rely fundamentally on
principles of cut and fill. Accurate topographic contours of current
conditions form the basis for understanding and reconfiguring
elevation at each individual site. By taking advantage of existing
topographic features, changes are surgically and efficiently merged
with the landscape.

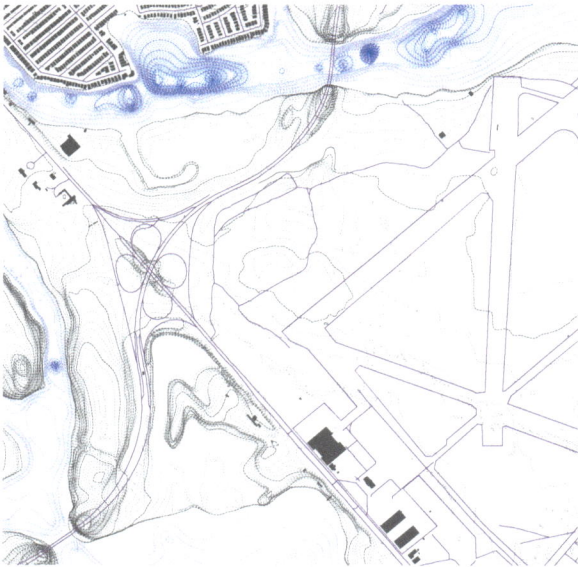

Existing contours, Floyd Bennett Marsh Inlet

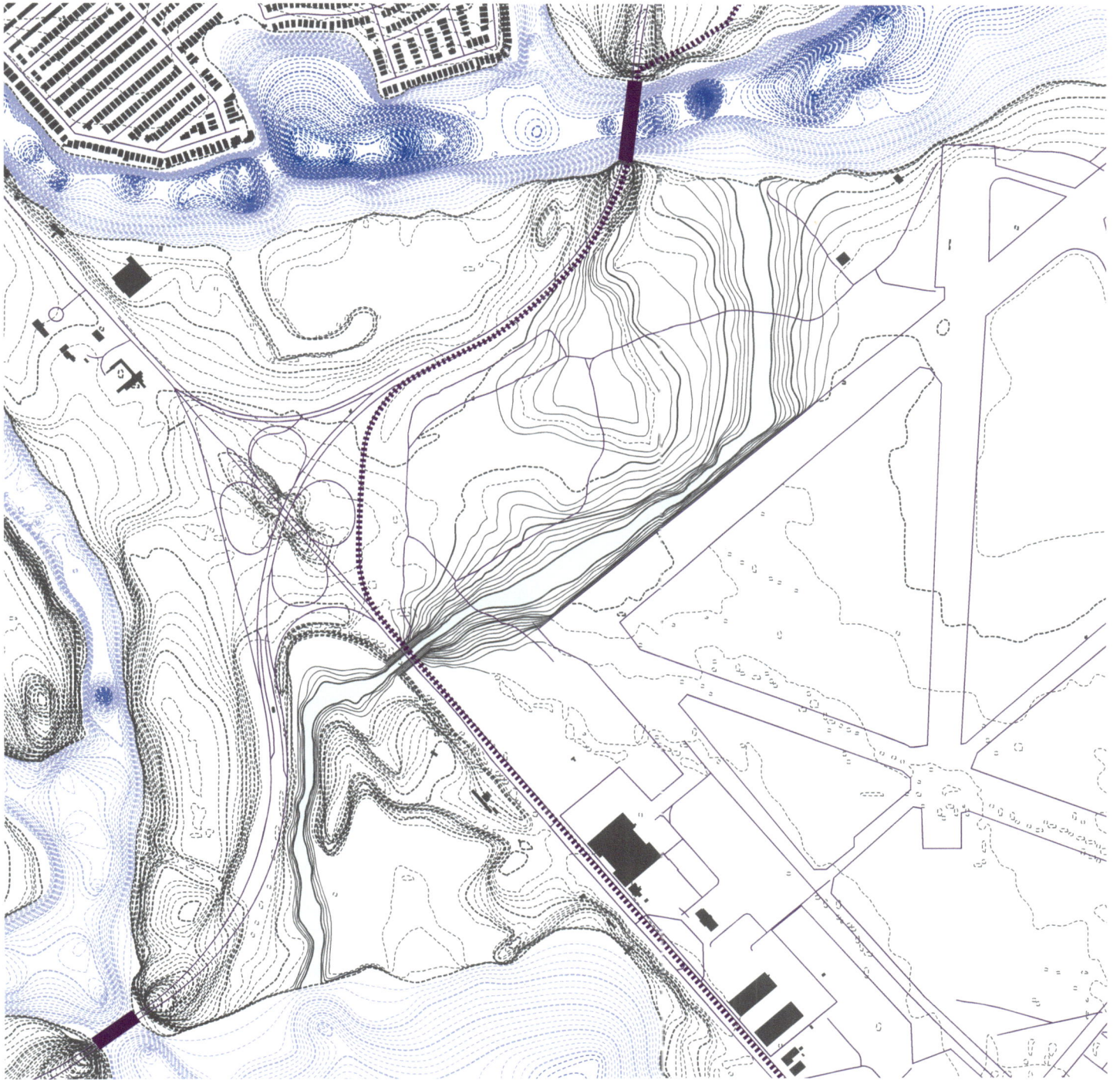

Proposed contours, Floyd Bennett Marsh Inlet

THE IMPORTANT OF FINDING ZERO: DESIGN AND VERIFICATION

PHYSICAL MODELING FROM TOPOGRAPHIC CONTOURS

A detailed project morphology has been developed at Jamaica Bay, from the regional scale of the watershed to local features within the embayment, through the use of physical models. Model construction methods include topographic contour models, glycerine soap casts of inverse contour models, and continuous-surface topobathy Computer Numerical Control (CNC) milled models.

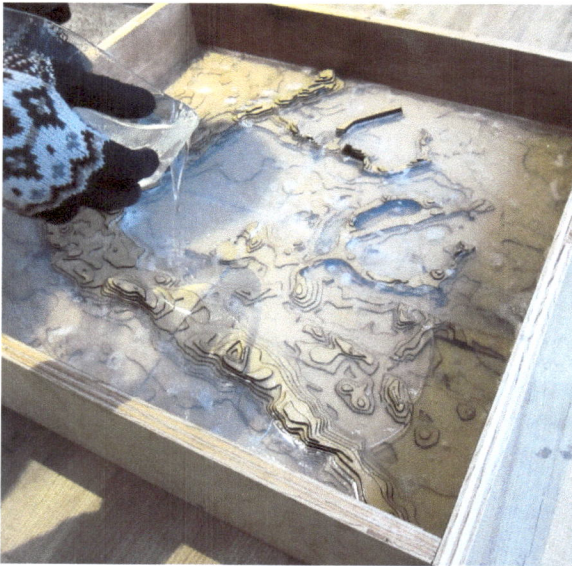

Floyd Bennett Inlet soap-cast physical model construction

Topographic contours generated from the merged DEM are used to produce laser-cut contour models

THE IMPORTANT OF FINDING ZERO: DESIGN AND VERIFICATION

PHYSICAL MODELING FROM TOPOGRAPHIC CONTOURS

These physical models are deployed in water tanks with injected dye to test the dynamic conditions of water flow, residence time, overwash, sediment transfer, and surge. The water tank studies have provided integral feedback to the design process at the full scale of the embayment as well as at detailed areas of interest.

JFK Runway flushing tunnel soap-cast model

CNC milled model and soap cast models generated from topographic contours

THE IMPORTANT OF FINDING ZERO: DESIGN AND VERIFICATION

PREDICTIVE MODELING WITH A DEM

An accurate DEM, among other input parameters, is the foundation for demonstrating possible future scenarios using digital models. A variety of predictive computer models rely on Digital Elevation Models to estimate future scenerios such as flooding from storm surge (SLOSH and ADCIRC), risk of wave impact at the shoreline (FETCH), storm surge attenuation by vegetation (CH3D), gradual inundation from sea level rise and ecosystem evolution with climate change over time (SLAMM), sediment movement and accumulation (PTM), and hydrologic flow dynamics (HydroQual).

The DEM can also be digitally modified to reflect design proposals and tested again to compare results before and after the proposed interventions.

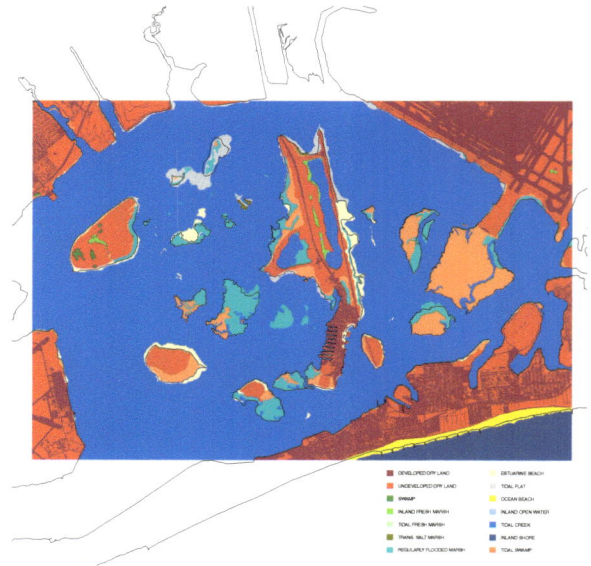

SLAMM Raster: Projected 2100 Marsh Migration

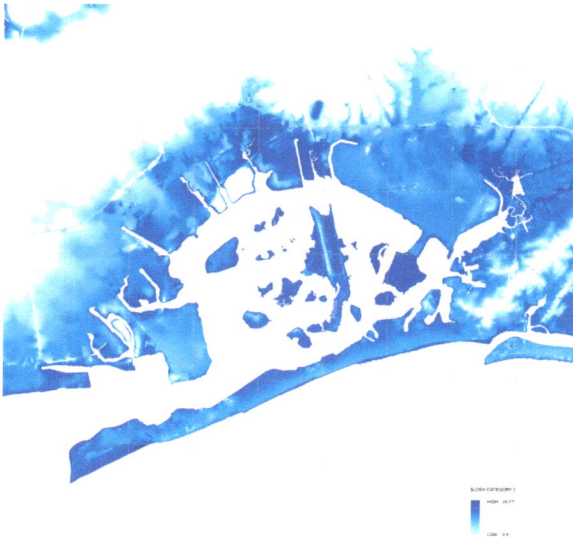

SLOSH Raster of Category 3 MOM Surge

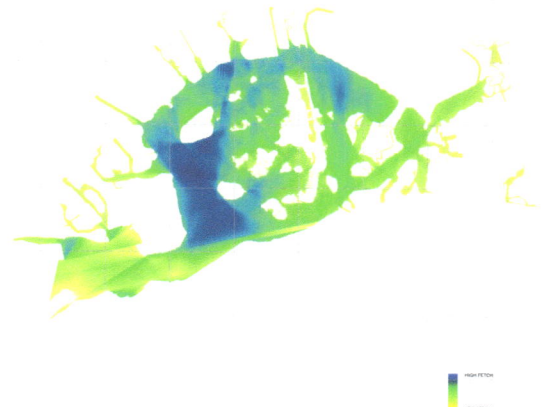

WAVES2012 Wind / Wave Fetch Raster

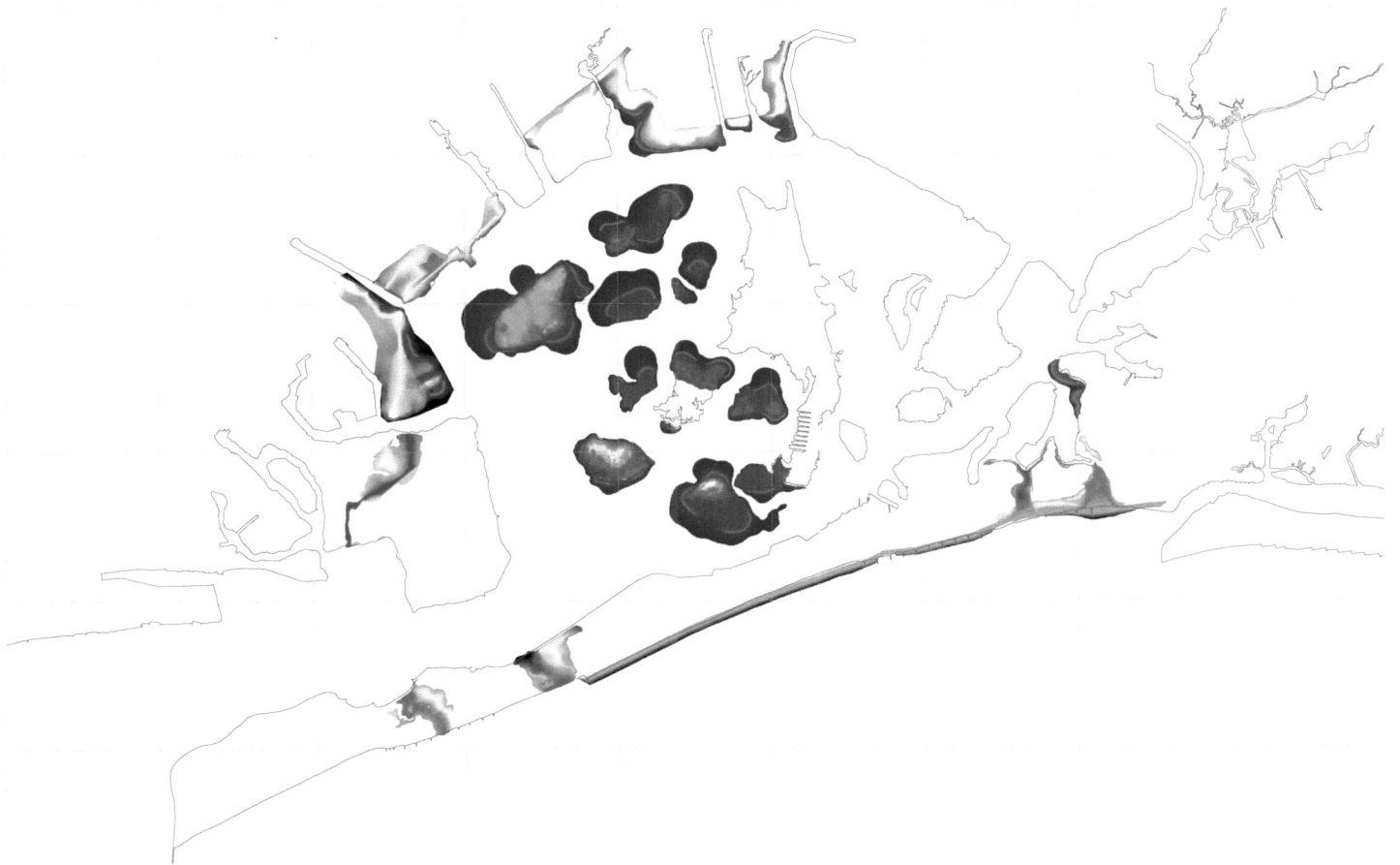

Modifications to the DEM representing proposed interventions, shown with existing shoreline

FINDING ZERO

PROCESS OVERVIEW

I.   Acquire shoreline

II.   Refine shoreline

III.   Acquire topographic data

IV.   Choose appropriate topographic data based on imaging technology, coverage, resolution, source date

V.   Merge selected topographic datasets

VI.   Acquire bathymetric data points

VII.   Refine bathymetric data

VIII.   Adjust bathymetric vertical datum

IX.   Transform bathymetric data from points to raster

X.   Clip topographic and bathymetric datasets to shoreline ("0")

XI.   Mosaic to a new raster, creating the merged topobathy DEM

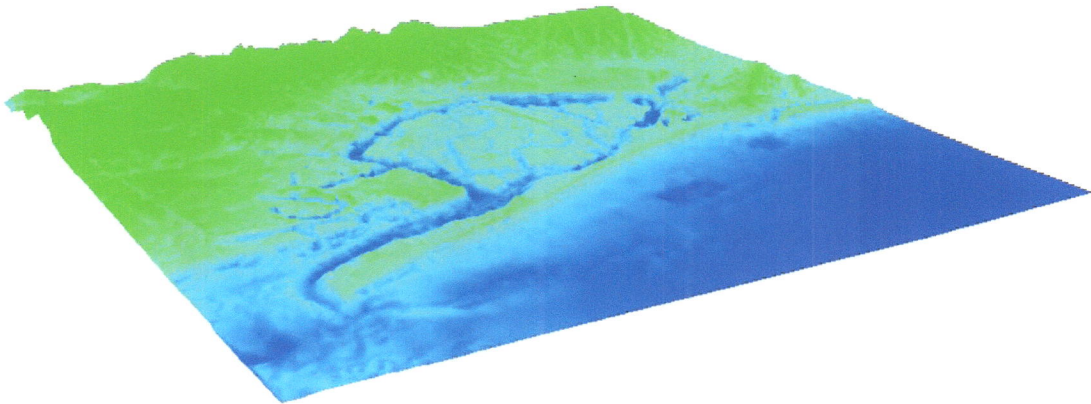

To visually represent the continuous land-to-water surface, digital elevation data of the land topography (referenced to the geodetic datum 1988 North American Vertical Datum, or NAVD 88) is merged with bathymetric point soundings from NOAA (referenced to the tidal datum Mean Lower Low Water, or MLLW). Given their different vertical datums, the challenge is finding the precise plane at which the topographic and bathymetric datasets meet: zero.

SHORELINE DATASETS

The shoreline serves as the seam between topographic and bathymetric datasets. For the datasets to stitch together smoothly, the shoreline must represent the same point in space relative to each. It must be "0" relative to NAVD 88 to correspond with the topographic DEM, and it also must be at approximately mean tide to correspond with the adjusted "0" of the bathymetric DEM.

The Water Line from FEMA's 2013 Preliminary Work Maps for the region corresponds to the NAVD 88 "0." Compared with the Hudson River Estuary Shoreline (2004), provided by New York State Department of Environmental Conservation Hudson Estuary Program and originally produced by Lamont-Doherthy Earth Observatory of Columbia University, FEMA's waterline is much more precise.

This line served as the base for building a complete edge within the scope of this project. Where the line was incomplete, we traced over aerial imagery and NOAA chart 12350 (2011) to make it continuous. Additionally, we incorporated the new "0" around recent marsh restoration footprints based on US Army Corps of Engineers project plan drawings.

NYSDEC Hudson River Estuary Shoreline, 2004

Original FEMA preliminary FIRM shoreline, 2013

FEMA preliminary FIRM shoreline, 2013, with adjustments

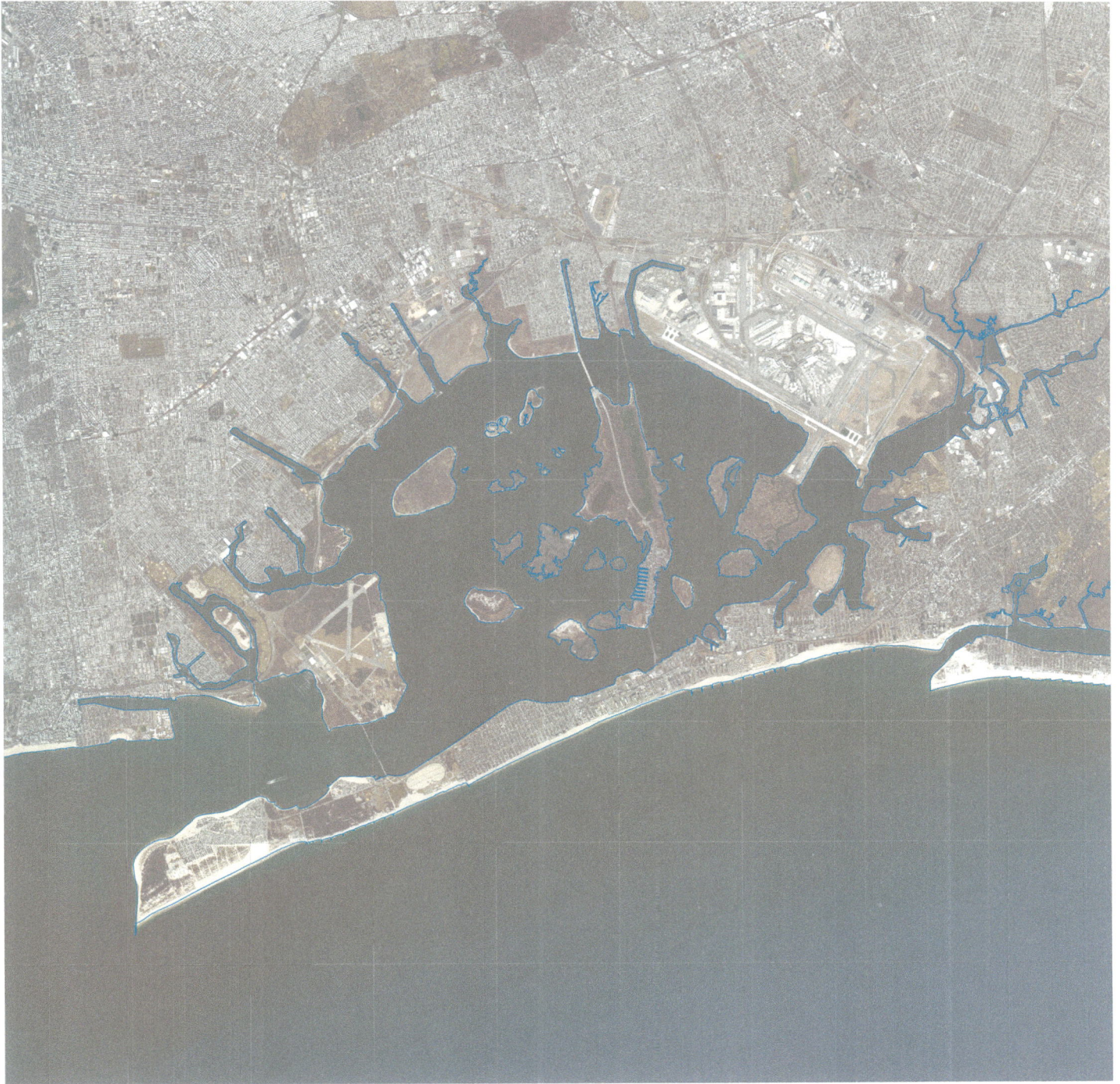

Revised shoreline: NAVD 88 "0"

TOPOGRAPHIC DATASETS

Topographic data can be freely acquired from a number of public sources including the USGS National Geologic Map Database, the New York State GIS Clearinghouse, and the New York City Open Data Catalog.

After comparing the coverage, resolution, date, imaging technology and corrections of different datasets we chose those most appropriate to the scope and resolution of this project, the National Map NED 1/3 (for New York City) and NED 1/9 (for Nassau County). These were merged and extraneous data "noise" was removed. This new topographic dataset was then further refined to reflect recent changes in key locations based on US Army Corps of Engineers project plan drawings, aerial imagery, and the New York City two-foot contour dataset.

New York City LIDAR (top)

resolution: 1 ft
date: 2010

* excludes parts of Nassau County
* resolution too fine for initial scale of project
* contours from this dataset unmanageable
* "bare earth" noise

National Map NED 1/3 (New York City) (center)

resolution: ~33 ft
source: USGS National Geologic Map Database
date: December 2011

* complete coverage of project scope including New York City and Nassau County
* this dataset produces manageable contours

National Map NED 1/9 (Nassau County) (bottom)

resolution: ~10 ft
source: USGS National Geologic Map Database
date: December 2011

* merged with NED 1/3 to create complete dataset with improved resolution where available

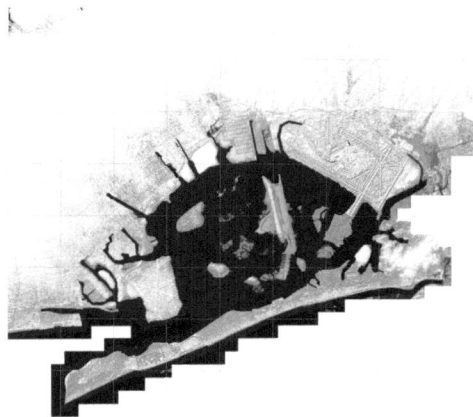

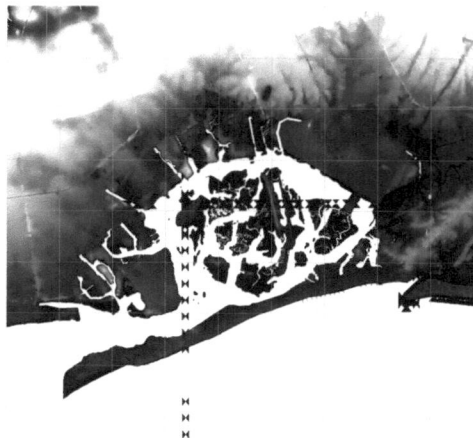

New York City two-foot contours

source: New York City Open Data Catalog

date: 2006

- used as reference to verify accuracy of contours produced from newly merged topographic datasets
- used to fill in missing Fountain Avenue Landfill elevations
- excludes Nassau County
- contour line format
- older dataset

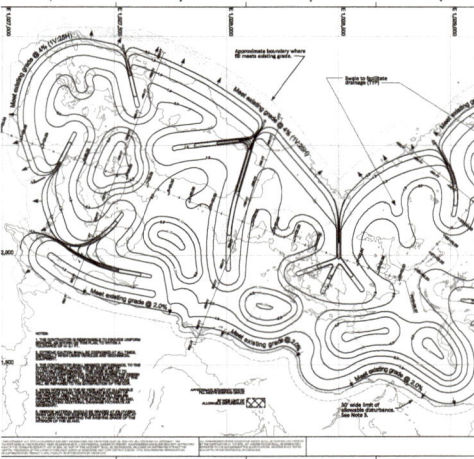

Contour Plan Drawings

source: US Army Corps of Engineers

date: 2006-2012

- used to incorporate newly restored marsh islands
  - Elders Point East (2006)
  - Elders Point West (2009-2010)
  - Yellow Bar Hassock (2012)
  - Black Wall Hassock (2012)
  - Rulers Bar Hassock (2012)

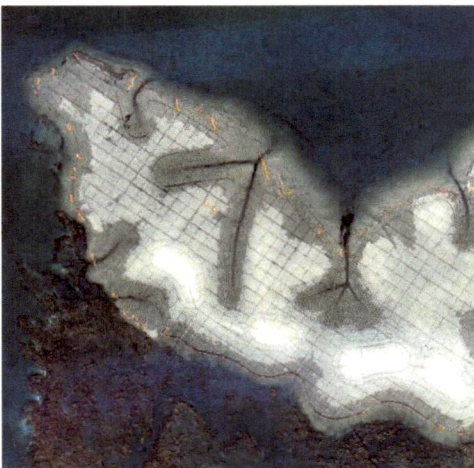

Aerial Imagery

source: Google Earth

date: 2012

- used to verify newly restored marsh islands
  - Elders Point East
  - Elders Point West
  - Yellow Bar Hassock
  - Black Wall Hassock
  - Rulers Bar Hassock

BUILDING THE TOPOGRAPHIC DEM

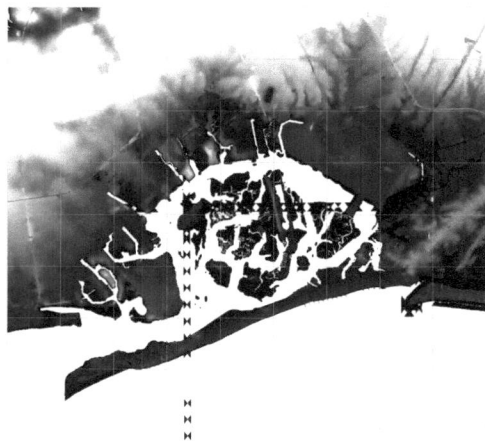

NED 1/3 (New York City)

NED 1/9 (Nassau County)

Refine Fountain Avenue Landfill, restored marsh island footprints

Clip out noise with refined shoreline

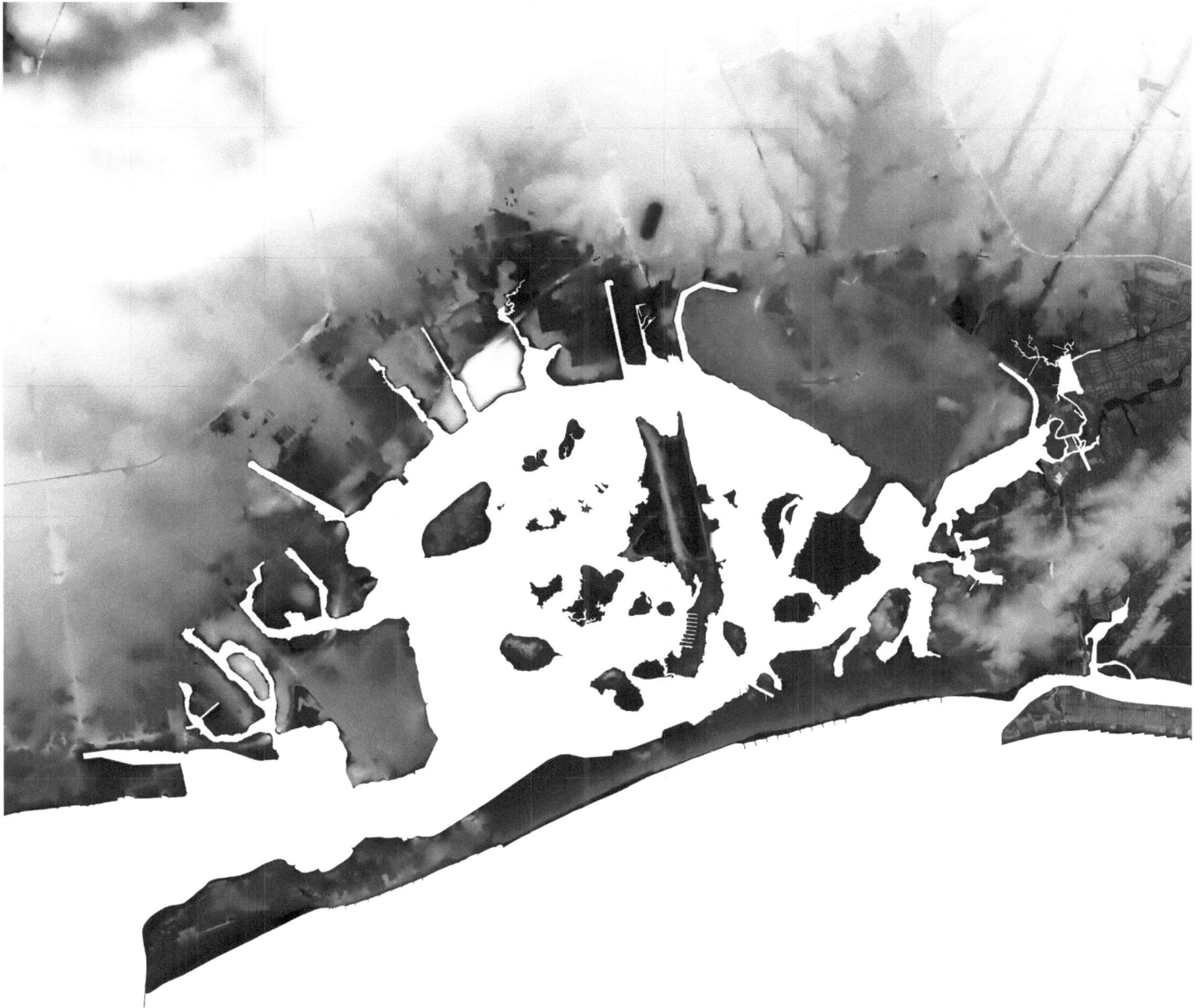

Topographic DEM

BATHYMETRIC DATASETS

Bathymetric soundings and charts can be freely acquired from NOAA's Electronic Navigational Chart website. FEMA's merged bathymetric - topographic model was produced by Production and Technical Services contractor Risk Assessment, Mapping and Planning Partners (RAMPP). This dataset is publicly available upon request. Additionally, the National Park Service commissioned Stoneybrook University to produce bethic scans within Jamaica Bay, which were carried out between 2003 and 2009.

For the purposes of this project, NOAA's soundings had the most complete coverage and enabled the refinement we needed. These sounding depths were interpolated in the tidal zone and adjusted to be relative to NAVD 88 "0."

NOAA chart 12350 (chart top right, point dataset center right)

resolution:	varies, approx 100 - 300 ft
source:	NOAA
date:	soundings from 2011 combined with historic soundings

- outline of mudflats (green) used as indicators of MLLW
- points with value of -2.82 added at this line and points with value of 0 added to mean tide line (yellow) to produce smooth representation of tidal flats

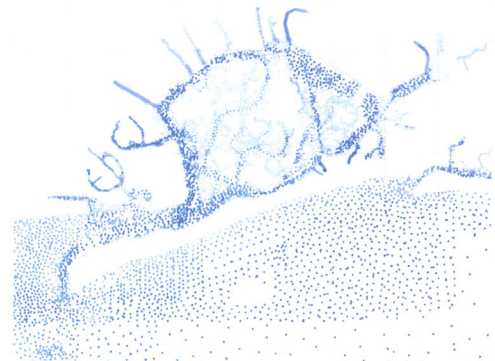

FEMA merged topo-bathy (bottom right)

resolution:	86.8 ft
source:	FEMA and RAMPP
date:	2011

- excludes land heights above +30 ft
- excludes ocean depths below -50 ft
- vertical datum adjustment may be inaccurate
- used as reference to compare with bathymetry raster produced from NOAA soundings

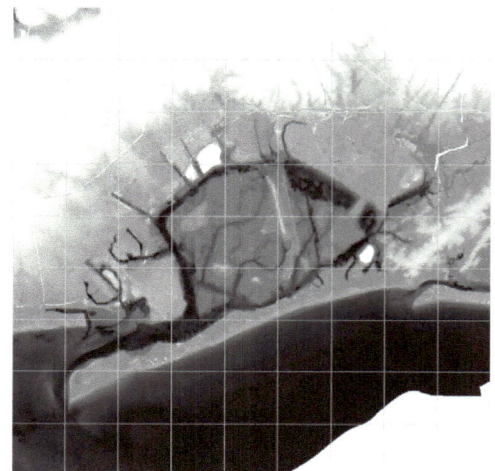

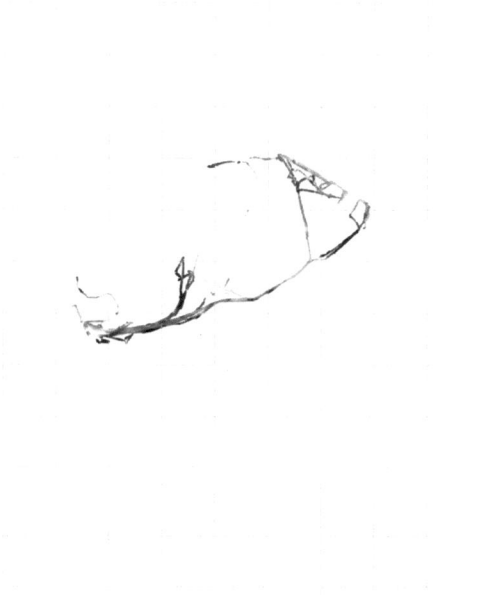

National Parks Service bathymetry scans
resolution: 1m
source: National Park Service
date: 2003 - 2009

• coverage of select channels only

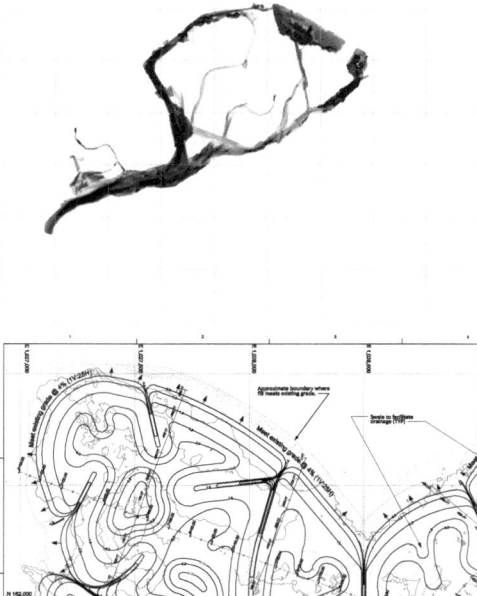

National Parks Service bathymetry scans
resolution: 5m
source: National Park Service
date: 2003 - 2009

• coverage not complete
• used as reference to compare with bathymetry raster produced from NOAA soundings

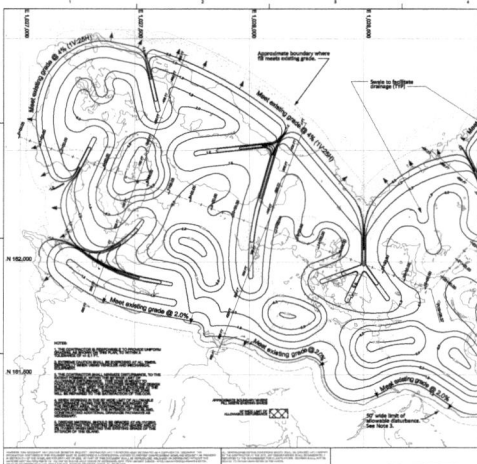

Contour Plan Drawings
source: US Army Corps of Engineers
date: 2006-2012

• used to incorporate newly restored marsh islands
    - Elders Point East   (2006)
    - Elders Point West   (2009-2010)
    - Yellow Bar Hassock (2012)
    - Black Wall Hassock   (2012)
    - Rulers Bar Hassock   (2012)

CREATING A REPRESENTATIVE BATHYMETRIC DATASET

INTERTIDAL ZONE REFINEMENT PROCESS

Given our goal of designing a "shovel ready" strategy for sequential dredged material placement and to encourage marsh island accretion, it was important to create a realistic representation of the sensitive intertidal zone where broad swaths of *Spartina alterniflora* marsh grasses exist. No merged digital elevation model existed that was accurate enough in the intertidal range for our purposes.

When representing large areas with very slight elevation change, small vertical increments in section will appear dramatically different in plan. As we tested different methods and datasets in our initial studies, the contours in the intertidal range fluctuated wildly. Previous iterations of the merged DEM produced unlikely contour configurations and a "wall" condition formed where there should have been a smooth gradient tidal flat.

Given the effect this would have on the ability to correctly calculate volumes of dredged material as required by the design proposals, it was critical to address these discrepancies.

Contours from intial DEM resulted in inaccurate representation of tidal zone and steep edge condition at tidal flat.

Contours from refined DEM result in smoth representation of tidal zone.

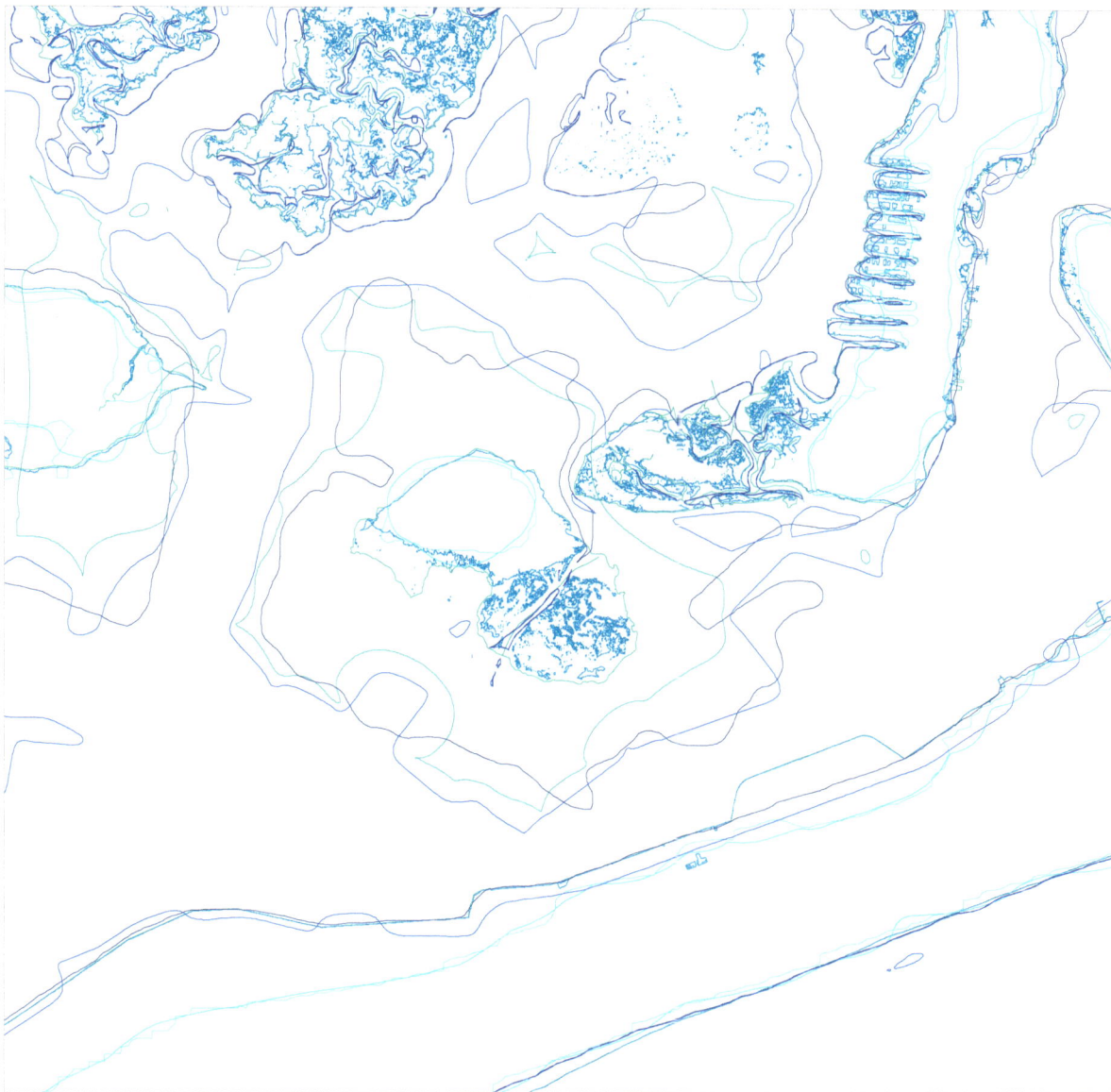

Conflicting lines of "0" produced from different datasets

CREATING A REPRESENTATIVE BATHYMETRIC DATASET

INTERTIDAL ZONE REFINEMENT PROCESS

Using the FEMA waterline, the NOAA ENC sounding point dataset from chart 12350, and the georeferenced image of NOAA chart 12350, two new new sets of points are created and merged with the original ENC sounding point dataset.

The shoreline (NAVD 88 "0") is converted from polygon to points, which are given a Z value of "0."

Additional points are entered manually using the georeferenced chart. Points are added precisely at the mudflat boundary (between green and blue). These are given a value of "-2.82," or the difference between NAVD88 "0" and MLLW at this location according to the nearest official NOAA tidal gauge at Sandy Hook.

These two new sets of points are merged. These combined points are then merged with the original ENC sounding point dataset.

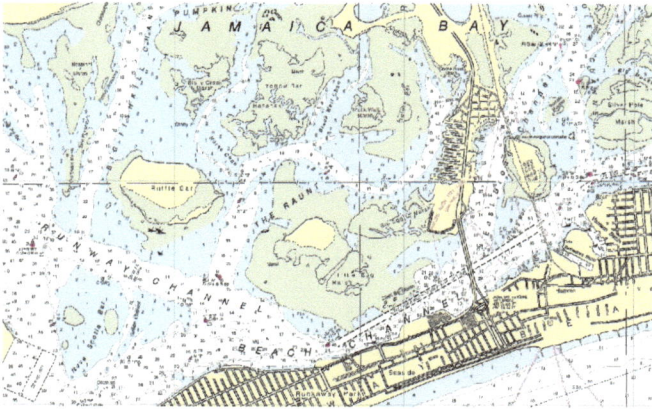

NOAA soundings, 2011, chart 12350

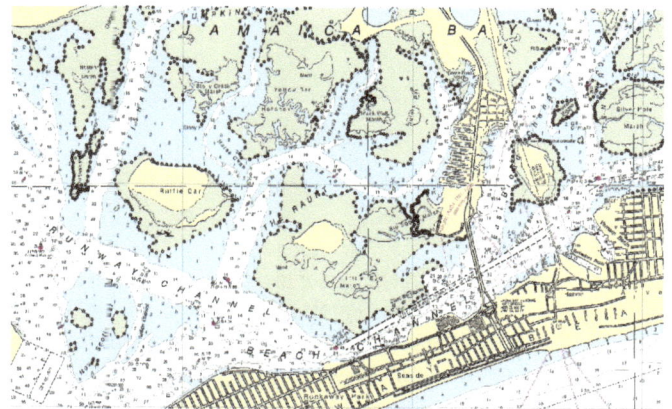

Manually input new points at MLLW using georeferenced NOAA navigational chart (new points get z value of -2.82 relative to NAVD 88 "0")

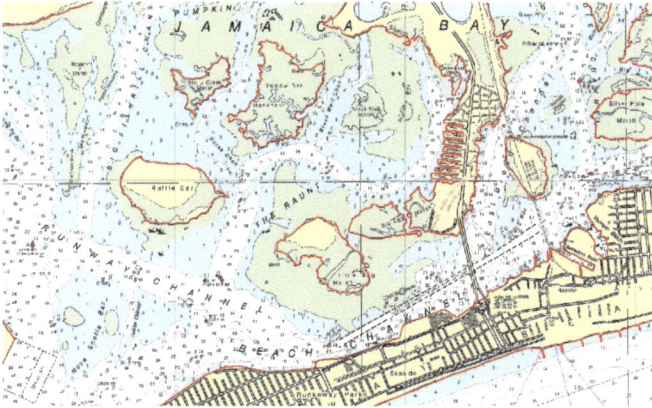

FEMA waterline (red) = NAVD 88 "0"

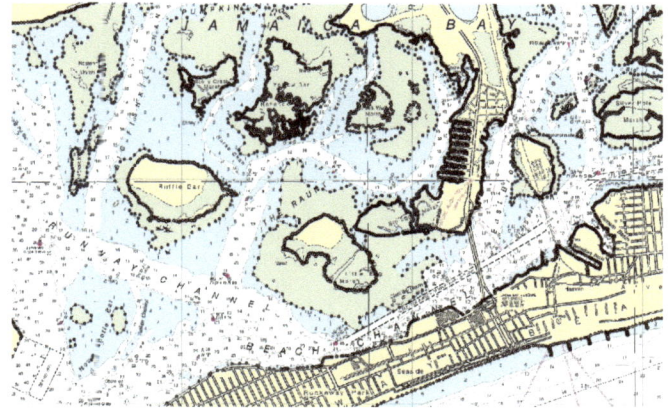

Combine new points: -2.82 (MLLW) and 0 (NAVD 88)

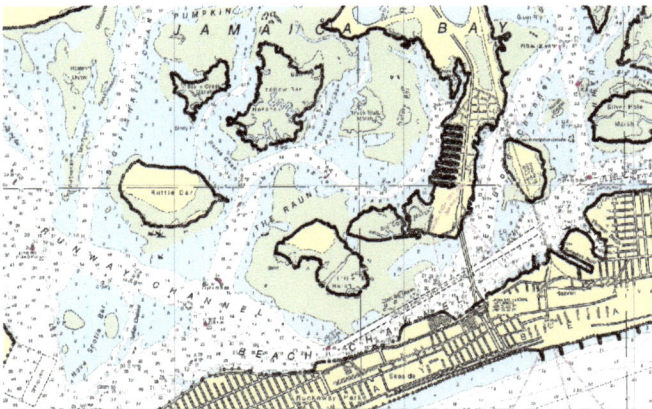

Convert FEMA "0" shoreline to points using ArcGIS 'feature vertices to points' tool (give points a Z value of NAVD 88 "0")

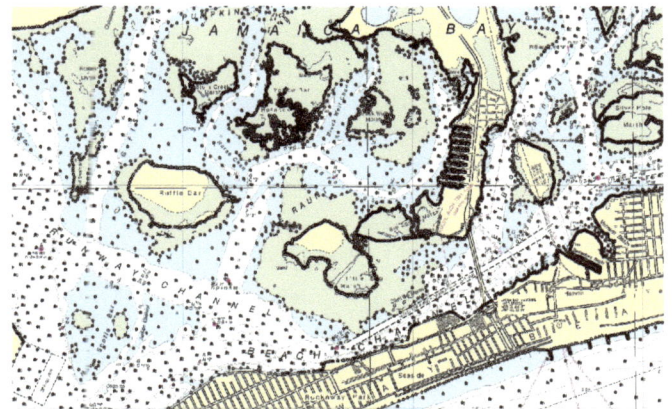

Merge new 0 and -2.82 (MLLW) points with adjusted NOAA ENC sounding dataset

CREATING A REPRESENTATIVE BATHYMETRIC DATASET

INTERTIDAL ZONE REFINEMENT PROCESS

The Esri ArcGIS Natural Neighbor tool then interpolates a surface from the new point dataset to produce a smooth representation of the entire bathymetry of the bay, including the tidal flats. Contours from this improved raster are smooth and do not create a wall.

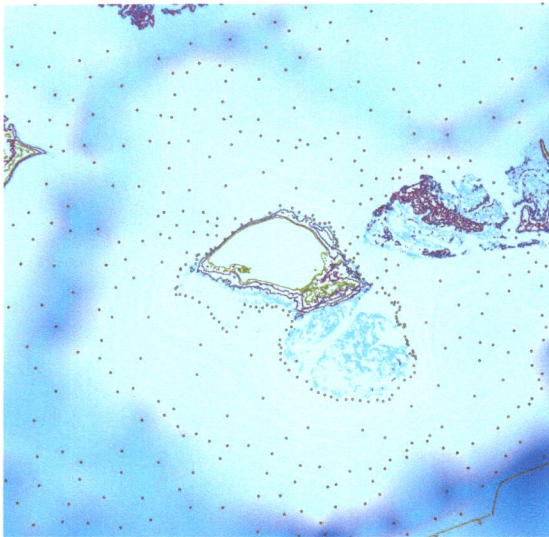

Points converted to raster

-3 to +3 contours delineating mudflats and key tidal wetland zone

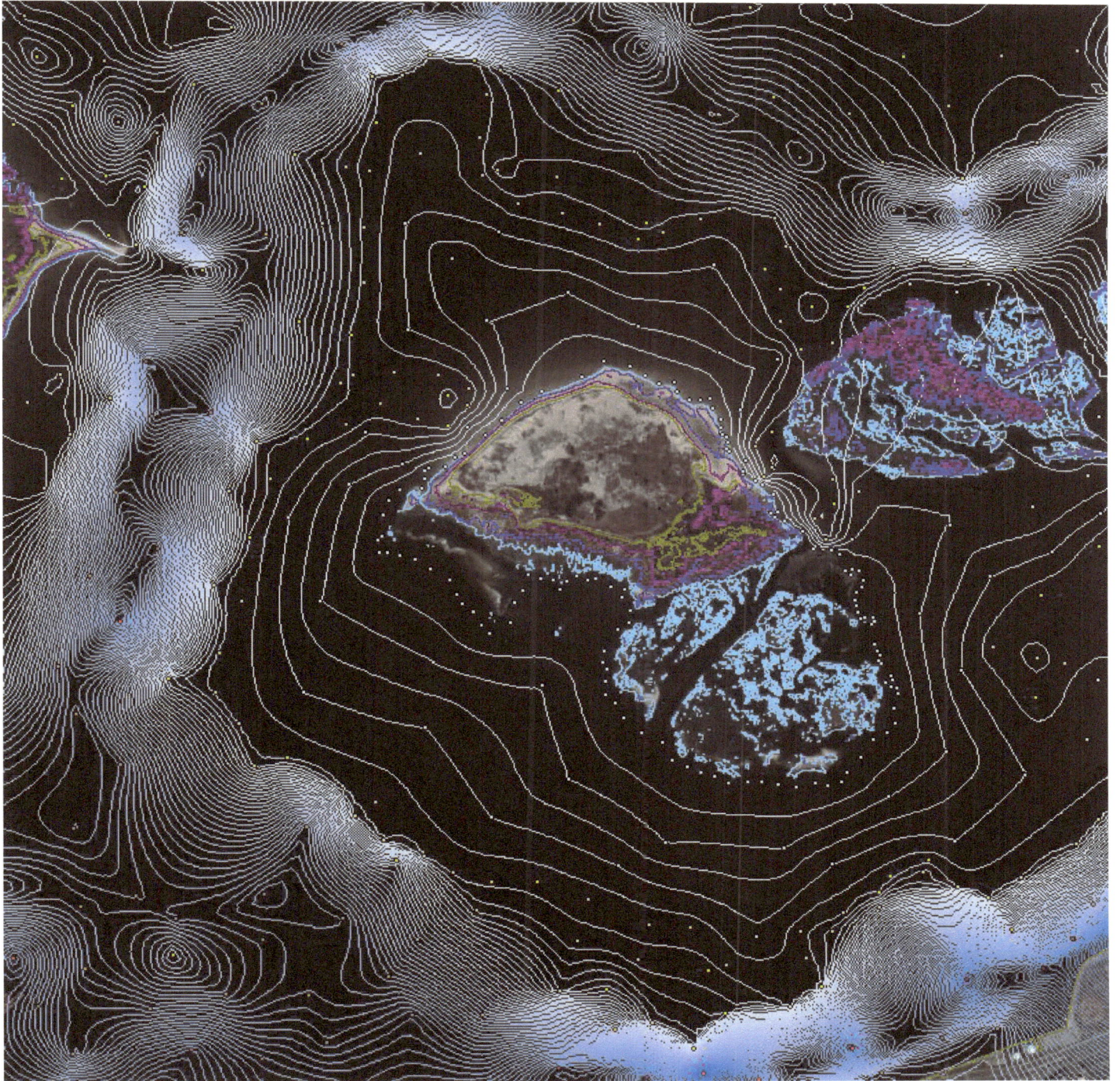

Aerial image with contours from new seamless raster

CREATING A REPRESENTATIVE BATHYMETRIC DATASET

ADJUSTING SOUNDING DEPTHS (TIDAL DATUM) RELATIVE TO GEODETIC DATUM (NAVD 88)

Bathymetric point soundings are referenced to the tidal datum Mean Lower Low Water, or MLLW. In order to make it relative to the geodetic datum NAVD 88, the difference between the two datums must be subtracted from the sounding depths. These points are deeper relative to NAVD 88 "0." Using the Sandy Hook tide gauge, the nearest official NOAA tidal station, this difference is -2.82. For example, a NOAA sounding with a depth relative to MLLW of -5 becomes -7.82 relative to NAVD 88 "0."

Performing this uniform calculation for all points within the scope of the Jamaica Bay study area is within a small margin of error. However, a more precise methodology is to use NOAA's VDatum point adjustment to correct for the tidal range variations, especially if working at a scale greater than that of Jamaica Bay. Within the scope of this project there were five adjustment zones, each with its own difference between NAVD 88 "0" and MLLW.

VDATUM adjustment ranges for Jamaica Bay area

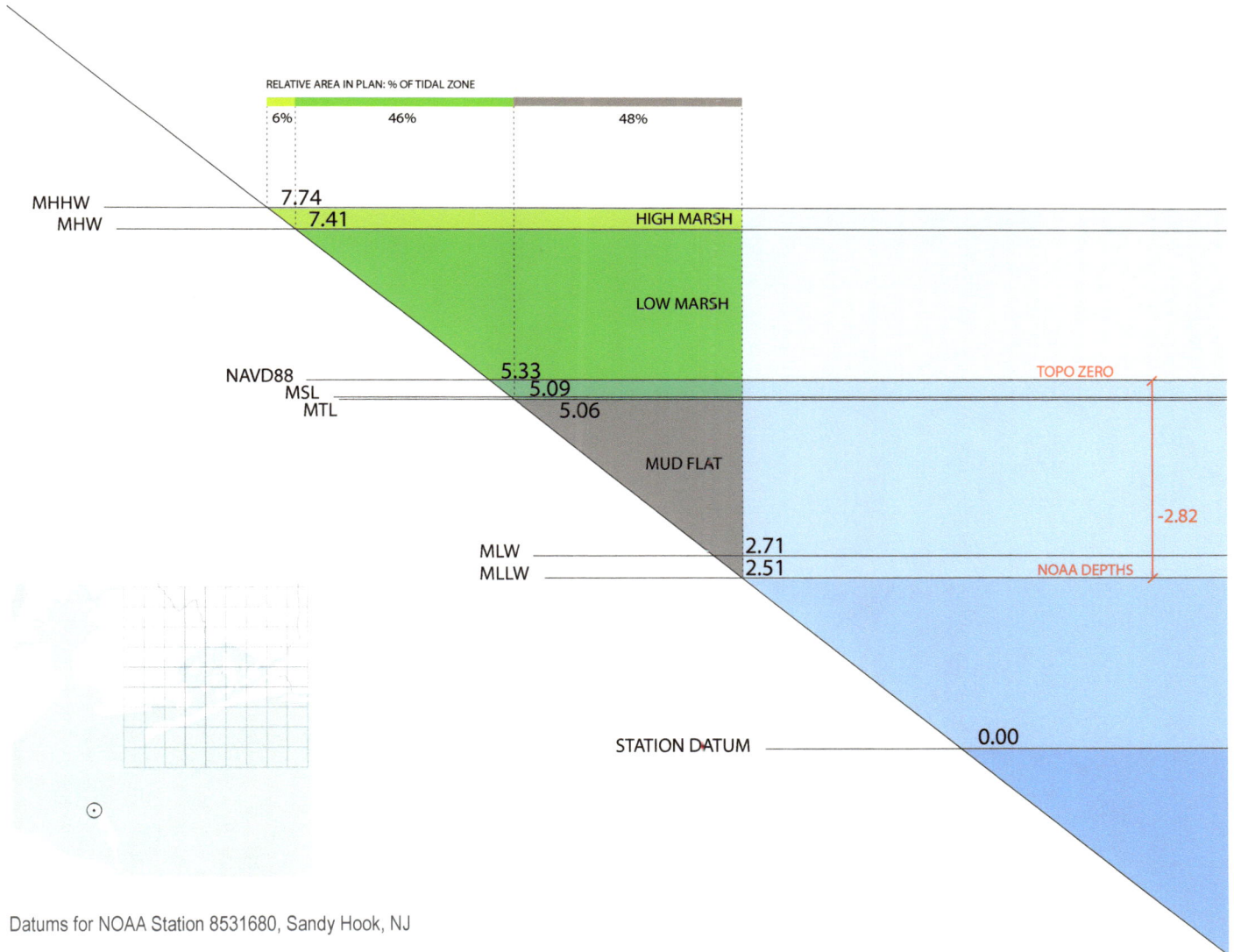

RELATIVE AREA IN PLAN: % OF TIDAL ZONE

6% | 46% | 48%

MHHW — 7.74

MHW — 7.41 — HIGH MARSH

LOW MARSH

NAVD88 — 5.33

MSL — 5.09

MTL — 5.06

TOPO ZERO

MUD FLAT

MLW — 2.71

MLLW — 2.51 — NOAA DEPTHS

-2.82

STATION DATUM — 0.00

Datums for NOAA Station 8531680, Sandy Hook, NJ

BUILDING THE BATHYMETRIC DEM

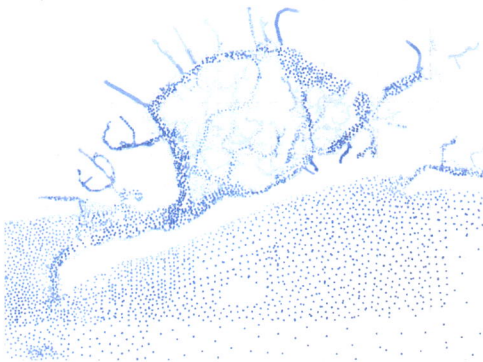

Complete bathymetric sounding point dataset

ArcGIS Natural Neighbor function 'Feature to Raster'
(detail of marsh islands and Broad Channel)

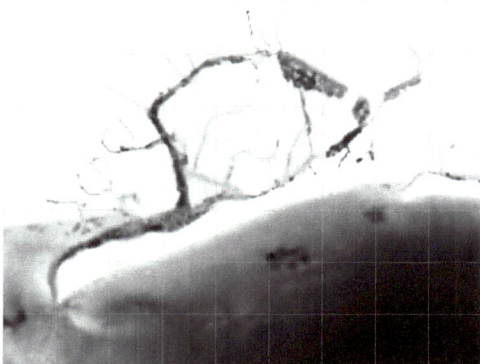

Bathymetric DEM prior to clipping

Clip new bathymetric DEM to shoreline

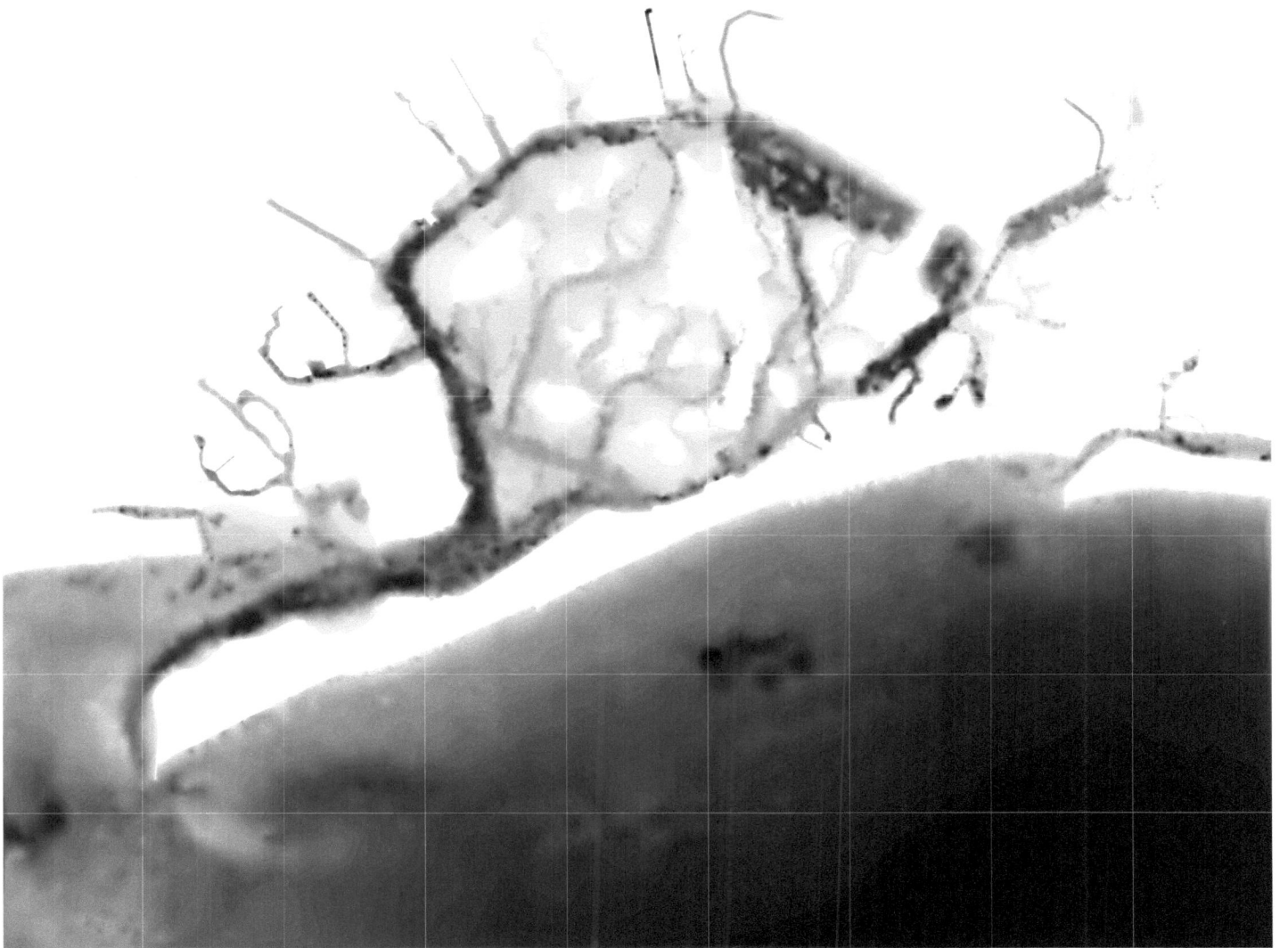

Bathymetric DEM

BUILDING THE MERGED TOPOBATHY DEM

MOSAIC TO NEW RASTER

The Esri ArcGIS Mosaic to New Raster tool combines the bathymetry and topography rasters into a single seamless merged model.

Topographic DEM

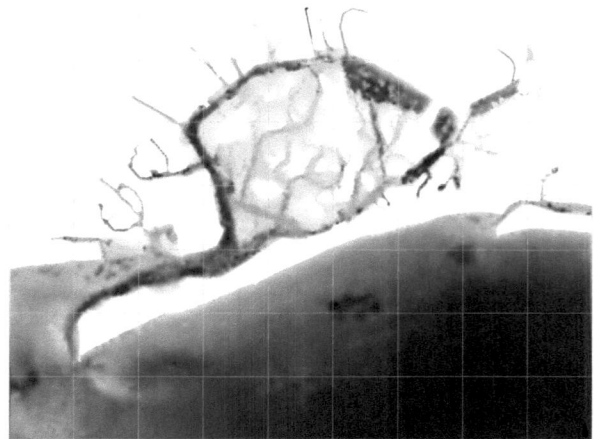

Bathymetric DEM

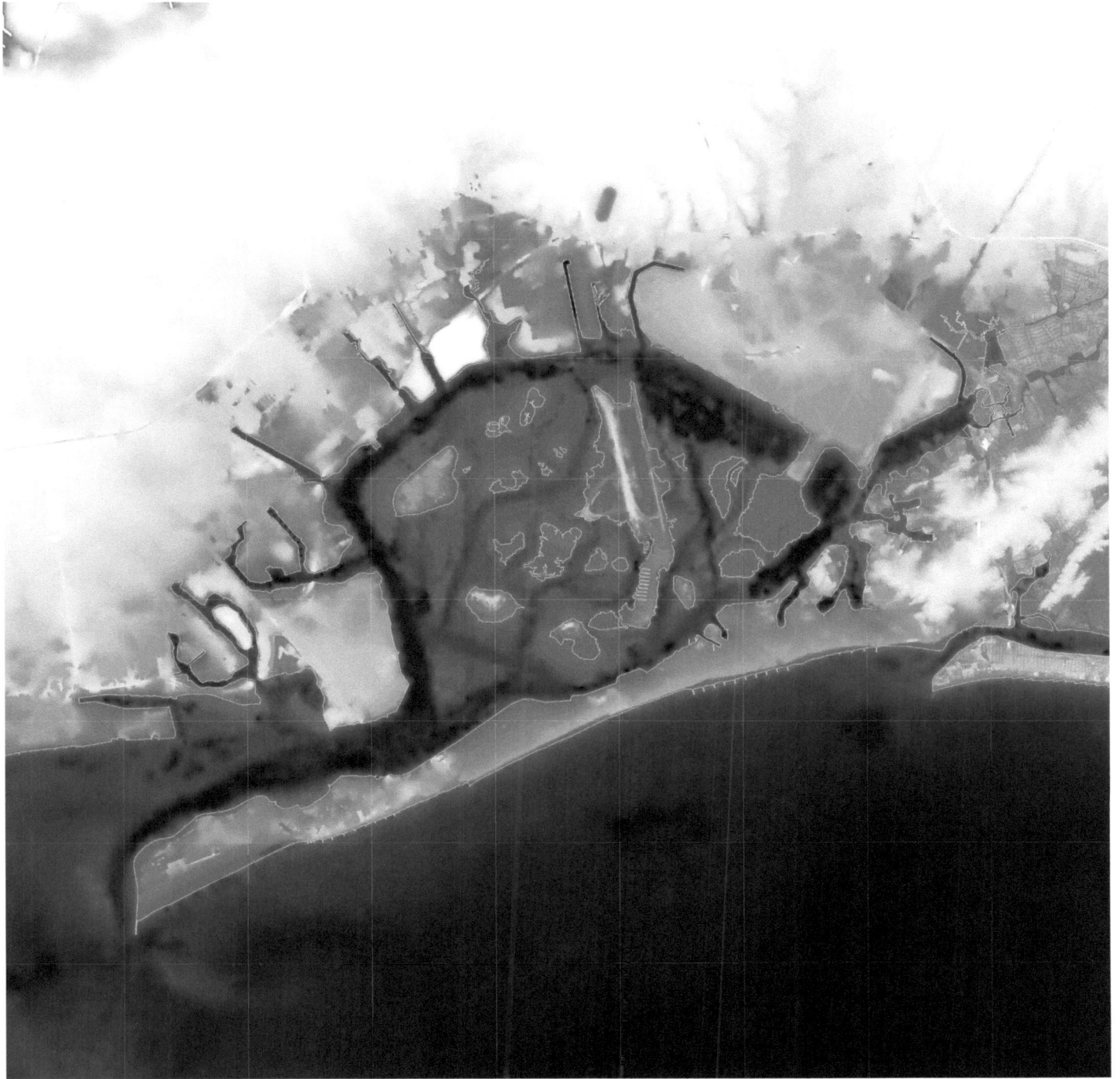

Merged Topobathy Digital Elevation Model with shoreline ("0")

www.ingramcontent.com/pod-product-compliance
Lightning Source LLC
Chambersburg PA
CBHW060826270326
41931CB00002B/76